LOVE IS LIFE

KAYSON PEARSON

Order this book online at www.trafford.com
or email orders@trafford.com

Most Trafford titles are also available at major online book retailers.

Print information available on the last page.

ISBN: 978-1-6987-0919-2 (sc)
ISBN: 978-1-6987-0921-5 (hc)
ISBN: 978-1-6987-0920-8 (e)

Library of Congress Control Number: 2021917409

Trafford rev. 08/23/2021

www.trafford.com
North America & international
toll-free: 844-688-6899 (USA & Canada)
fax: 812 355 4082

CONTENTS

DEDICATION

This is dedicated to ALL the QUEENS in my life!
To the Queens who I have lost and are no longer here:
The Queen of Queens; My Mother Sandra Faye Pearson
Bridget "Granny" Hinds, Betty "MaMa" Pearson, Inez "Great Grandma" Pearson
Aunt Anita Pearson and Aunt Joyce Hinds

To the Queens who are still here:
Nekiya Pearson, Marion "Liz" Pearson, Lorretta Grant
Sean-Ashley, Unique, Kiera, Darrienne, Sandra "Sandy", Shawnna "Tipsy", Damani
Aunt Rita, Aunt Debra, Aunt Robin, Aunt Hazel
Risse, Lene, Kewanda, Shataun, Shirl, Lateak, Denisha, Angie, Quana, Precious

To the Queens I have loved, and the Queens I Dream I could love:
Venecia Cobble, Fatima "Dameli" Moore, Uniqua Smith, Lakeya Artis
Jhene Aiko, Gabriel Union, Sade, Monica, Taraji P. Henson, Tatianna Ali, H.E.R
Rihanna, Harley Dean, Nautica Thorn, Jessica Alba, Sarah Hyland

I PRAY, THAT WITH THIS DEDICATION AND THESE HANDS OF A KING, THAT I HAVE BUILT FOR ALL YOU QUEENS, A THRONE OF IMMORTALITY! MAY OUR NAMES BE FOREVER BOUND AND LIVE ON ETERNALLY IN THE HEART, MIND AND SOUL OF THE UNIVERSE!!!

The Last Kiss

Lips cold as ice
    Flesh hard as steel
Hands white as rice
    Can this be real?
Yesterday was filled with life
    Today all is gone
Tomorrow sorrow will be rife
    Eventually life goes on
Life is strong
    Yet so fragile
Too late to right the wrong
    The body is no longer agile
Now sit and ponder this
    Are you prepared for that last kiss?

Idrissa

The beginning and the end
    Alpha and Omega
Finish to begin
    Kokowame au voohoria
Start to finish again
    In and out of gaia
A wheel that never cease to spin
    Idrissa! Idrissa! Idrissa!

I Promise

Give me your hand
I promise to make your every wish my command
Give me your body
I promise to deliver you pure ecstasy
Give me your mind
I promise to love you blind
Give me your heart
I promise our love will have no end nor start
Give me your soul
I promise to make us one whole
Just give me a single moment
I promise to us, forever!

My Butterfly Love

Taking this chance
    To express my feelings
My heart wants to dance
    With the love your dealing
Never did I imagine
    That the soul could kiss
Like an overdose of heroin
    A never ending bliss
I know I should
Kiss your lips with roses
Only if I could
    I'd part seas for you like Moses
I take deep breaths
    Knowing you share the same air
With the time I have left
    I'll work to keep you near
God's Gift to me
    The loveliest of land, sea, and sky
Queen of my heart's glee
    Loved by a beautiful butterfly!

My Favorite Pair Of Jeans

How did you get it in there
each soft, plump, firm basketball
Not just one, the whole pair
Got me whistling like a bird call

       How does something so tender and old
       Control something so young and hard
       Worshipping it like a idol of gold
       With priests always standing guard

     Time shaped it like an hour glass
     Dangerously curvy and lean
     Please tell me how did you get that ass,
     In them skin tight jeans?

I just love how they move with you
And they're my favorite hue of blue!

No Justice No Peace

Help! Help!
I can't breathe!
Don't shoot!
Their final pleas

Fucking coon!
Stop resisting!
Thought he had a gun!
Equals a justified lynching

Surely it rings a Bell
Whether your black or Brown
Just the devil out of his shell
Shots fired! Another nigger down

Ain't funny at all, no Martin
A grave of roses picked by a Gardner
No justice! No peace! Again and again
Doesn't get easy, just harder

Now the tables turn, what's the Mata
Can't believe it cause you police
Good news all over the blotter
Revenge! Pay back! The Big Brenski!

The Last Rose

If I gave a rose,
    for every time our lips kissed
If I gave a rose,
    for every moment we missed
If I gave a rose,
    for every pleasure we wished
If I gave a rose,
    for every time love we dismissed
If I gave a rose,
    Roses would cease to exist.

The Broken Heart

Once upon a time
A heart lay broken
No one paid it any mind
It's tale left unspoken
Through all the years
There it laid untouched
It's face a stream of tears
From being stepped on too much
Why wouldn't anyone fix it?
At least stop and say hi
Soon it was ready to quit
And wave the world good-bye
Then a hand reached out
Could this be a cruel dream
Surely the heart had it's doubts
A finger wiped it's teary stream
Hands and fingers caressed it gently
The heart lit up like a clown
Begging for more silently
Then it suddenly screamed, put me back down!

Crow Song

Hateful words are spoken
A heart left broken
A window is wide open
None saw the body floating
Only the dead truly know
The song of the lonely crow

Neglected for drugs
Feelings crushed like bugs
Drunken tears soak the rug
The lifeless trigger delivers the slug
Only the dead truly know
The song of the lonely crow

Pleasure is worst than pain
Scars from abuse still remain
Memories make this sane
As oxygen is cut off from the brain
Only the dead truly know
The song of the lonely crow

Dragon Rose

Kissed by fire
love born in hell
Ringed by the abominable choir
Looking into the eyes of El

Hell to the Queen
Darkness brightly chanted
Also known as Mary Magdalene
Before this throne she'd been granted

As below, so above
Could never be more true
Hands reaching for love
From darkness to a lighter hue

A garden of roses
Flourishing in the heat
A love the world opposes
Refusing to embrace defeat

Waiting until the world ends
High on her blazing throne
Girded by family and friends
Yet still all alone

When her King makes the call
She will truly have it all!

Stupid Cupid

I don't know of anyone more stupid
Than that cruel fucker Cupid
Why can't he take those arrows
And shove it up his ass
This way the effect and
Pain will be sure to last

Ol' stupid Cupid
And his idea of love
Is just so fucking stupid

Expletive Love

A heart no one can heal
It no longer beats
It no longer speaks
Most of it can no longer feel

An end that resonates who I'm to be
Although it's still inside
It's no longer alive
Therefore, no longer a part of me

Surely I'll never be the same
Though others may come along
And all the pain is gone
I'll only love with my brain

So is the end of my once loving heart
How to find love, where do even start?

Soul Raider

"I come in peace"
The first words of attack
Numbers began to decrease
Only amongst the blacks
They discovered a civilized people
And hid their savage nature
We treated them as our equal
Regardless of their skin's color
Divine knowledge we handed down
Cruel blades they thrusted up into our flesh
Unsacrificial blood painted the ground
The loved turned heartless
The creation turned on their creators
Oh! This you didn't know to be?
Surely it's written in the Holy Scriptures
Genesis, chapter 30, verses 31 to 43
Will the savages ever be repaid?
For stealing knowledge and stealing souls
Our ancestors' blood still stains their blades
Will we not rise up and take back control
What happened to the dark came to light
Your secrets of sacrilege are no longer hidden
Soon you'll know the lion's might
We're the Original, so who you kidding
"But, I come in peace!"
Yeah right! Those days are over
The awakened amongst our people has increased
We know you; savage child; soul raider!

Loving Memories

There was Tracy
From science class
She would let me
Experiment with her ass
In english literature
Was sweet Monique
I would let her
Act out le'frique
Stephanie Amstead
From home-ac
Got hotter than fresh bread
When I kissed her neck
Crystal Stall
From gym
Would grab my balls
And spit on them
Tonya, Deneise, and Jacquelynn
Would only french kiss
Latoya, Lanise, and Robin
Were freaks on cannabis
Janis, Justine, and Veronica
Only with my finger tips
Candice, Kristen, and Monica
Knew how to work their hips
Tulip, Trixie, and Shavon
Was afraid I would tell
Honey-Dip, Dixie, and Javon
Said I knew them so well
Danielle, Misty, and Winter
Left me blue and cold
Michelle, Christy, and Summer
Always something new and bold

All the girls
From way back then
Still share my world
Cause memories never end
Some times we did nothing
And at times all of the above
We all gave each other something
On our quest for love

Don't Cry

Step-dad said all good girls did it
Deep down you knew it was bad
Your mother called you a lying little bitch
Cause you resembled your real dad
Night after night your door would open
In came something worst than the Boogey Man
For it to stop you kept praying and hoping
Until you became numb to the touch of his hand
Through it all you managed to keep your pride
Though still battling those evil thoughts
A dark secret you keep deep inside
That somehow you thought it was your fault
The nightmares constantly return
You wonder when will the torture cease
In hell you wish for him to burn
But that still doesn't bring you peace
I can't imagine the pain you feel
To say I understand would be a complete lie
What I'm offering from my heart is real
A strong shoulder to lean on, and a tissue to dry your eyes!

Isn't She Lovely

Do you see the beauty of Mother?
How her green hair grows wild
Changing from one color to another
Do you dig her enchanting style?
Do you dream to her blood's flowing?
Eager to wash your feet
When it comes down crashing
Until the transformation is complete
Do you marvel at her majestic crown?
Reaching to the highest peaks
Or how her voice makes a wondrous sound
When she opens her mouth to speak
From the bottom to the top of thee
Isn't she lovely?

Lunatic

You give life to the night
Though engulfed in darkness
Still your smile shines bright
Not to stare I try my hardest
How can I ignore your beauty
When I've been waiting impatiently for you
To worship you is my duty
There's nothing in this universe more true
You only visit me thirteen times a year
Why is your love so cruel
Your last night I shed a tear
Surely I'm your fool
Why can't you stay forever
And bless me with your love
My life would be so much better
If you would never fall from above
What choices do I have
But to watch you slowly pass by
As I smile and laugh
And prepare for my last cry
I know you'll always come back
As the sun is sure to shine
With your mysterious enchanting beauty still intact
Just know you'll always be mine
My love it's time for our kiss farewell
We share a special kind of magick
Please be back before my soul leaves this shell
Until, I'll forever be your lunatic!

Keep It Jazzy

Give me something pure and simple
No vocals, just instrumentals
Let me hear the horns blaze loud and smooth
Something my soul can groove too
Let the drum beat vibrate my bones
Bringing me memories of home sweet home
As the piano mixes in with harmony
Now this is what I call groovy baby
Give me something that will forever last
Give me that sweet, soulful jazz!

Holla

Come one, come all
Come short, come tall
Come thick, come thin
Come any color of skin
Come, for I seek a friend

From woods to cities
From states to countries
From highs to lows
From castles to bungalows
I'll be awaiting your hellos

Whether young or very old
Whether shy or very bold
Whether shallow or very deep
Whether sour or very sweet
All I would like to meet

From east to west
At your worst or your best
From north to south
Whole lot to say or nothing to talk about
I want to receive your shout out
Age, race, faith, residence
All of these don't matter
So pick up a pen and paper
And don't hesitate to send me a letter!

Good-Bye All

Gone, gone, is the time
Long gone is the heart
Come back to the mind
Back, back, to the start

Nights, nights, remain dark
Cold nights with no star
Day light make your mark
Light, light, leave a scar

Death, death, claim your prize
Lone death embrace all
Sweet life clear your eyes
Life, life, heed their call

Long gone is the time
Gone, gone, no longer mine!

Live And Learn

It's like slow motion
Just coast'n
Flowing with the ocean
It's groovy baby

It's like being in love
For the first time
Having a broken heart
Was the worst time

It's like prolonging life
Only to die later
Going up and down
Like an elevator

It's like being born
And smacked by a stranger
No mother's protection
When your in danger

It's being kissed by the moon
Hugged by a star
Caressed by the sun
Everywhere you are

It's like dying without pain
But no mourns you
This life is something else
They could've warned you!

Cheating Heart

Your stories are filled with lies
All your words are deceptive
Breaking down in phony cries
My heart is no longer receptive
Your cheating heart makes you act this way
Your cheating heart is pushing love away

Your constant lusting for others
One no longer satisfies
Faithful you vowed to be to eachother
Promises you turned to lies
Your cheating heart is cold
Your cheating heart no one can hold

Deep down inside you want to love
You refuse to be hurt again
In your heart is a crying dove
Wishing for the pain to end
Your faithful heart was cheated on before
Your cheating heart knows faithful no more!

The Best Things Are Free

You and me
Laying under a tree
K-I-S-S-I-N-G
Enjoying the birds' melody
As the sun sets slowly
Introducing a night sky so starry
A full moon shines brightly
Mesmerizing is it's beauty
We're cuddled up all cozy
Laughing at how life can be
So damn crazy
Every moment for you you and me
Is like a magickal fantasy
We can be extremely wealthy
Or have no money
These things don't have a fee
Is it so hard to believe
That God intended for it to be
That the best things in L-I-F-E
Are free
Especially
When we're laying under a tree
F-U-C-K-I-N-G!

Endurance

This torture, I shall endure
The constant numbing pain
Give me, feed me, more and more
It will never teach my brain
What's behind this impenetrable door
Will always remain the same
So give me, feed me, more and more
I shall endure, I shall endure, I shall endure!

Shush

I fell off the fence
Bordering my sanity
Falling into silence

This waking somnolence
As I found harmony
I fell off the fence

With mind's obedience
I became a deity
Falling into silence

With great confidence
Underestimating gravity
I fell off the fence

Searching for my innocence
And humanity
Falling into silence

Tired of the nonsense
Walking away from vanity
I fell off the fence
Falling into silence

Only One

Did you thank your mother?
Hugged your son?
Forgave your father?
You know there's only one

Are you chasing your dreams?
Don't forget to enjoy and have fun
Dancing in the sun's beams
You know there's only one
Have you given love a chance?
Escaped a bullet from an angry gun?
Well here's your warning in advance
You know there's only one

What are you waiting for?
Every moment an opportunity has begun
To do all you dream and more
I won't tell you again, there's only one

Don't take for granted
What isn't an promise
For Father Time is a bandit
Stealing that only one... with a kiss!

Beautiful Rose

Beautiful you truly are
You, my eyes rejoice to see
Staring at the brightest star
A shinning star of beauty

Skin smooth as spring
A gentle cool breeze
Pleasure your touches bring
Unintentionally you aim to please

Eyes warm as summer
Burning heat of passion
Long days of wonder
Peaceful nights everlasting

Personality colorful as autumn
Radiantly bright and beautiful
Others fall to their end
You stand shinning and graceful

Smile white as winter
Glistening in the sun
Warm breathe is cooler
Competition failed, your number one

Beautiful are the flowers of earth
Your the one I chose
The word beauty, you gave birth
Your my one and only, beautiful rose!

Missing You

Nights are not dark
Mornings are not bright
If your not here for me to hold tight
Hawks don't seem to soar
Canaries don't seem to sing
Cause I want all of you or nothing
My heart doesn't beat on time
My brain doesn't function correctly
But when you are around everything works lovely
Without you everyday is a lie
Without you I can't tell what's false or true
All these things happen simply cause I'm missing you!

Thinking Of You

Sleep don't come easy
My breathing is wheezy
Heart drums to a thunderous beat
Tongue longing to taste your lustful sweets
I need you here so I can fly
Your lost presence brings tears to my eyes
I beg and plea to know when will it stop and when will it start
The insanity that comes from my heart
Thoughts that make me happy and sad I don't know what to do
Yet I love them all the same as I sit here thinking of you!

Through Love's Fire

Step into my heart and feel the heat
of passion that burns only for you
Close the door, so that the winds that
froze your heart will not come through
Feel the heat of the fire against your cold heart
as it melts all your fears and worries away
Know in your mind, body, and soul this is where you
belong and in my heart you will always stay
See the fire burning wildly, but you know
that it can do you no harm
Reach in and feel my love burning for you
although its hot, its soothingly warm
Now step all the way into
the core of my burning desire
Feel your mind, body, heart, and soul melt
into mines as we become one
    I am the inextinguishable fire!

Love's Treasure

Love is your only treasure
All else is lost to the world
You shine like stars and bees
Death only makes me want you more
Not even God can keep you from me
In dreams, your my reality
I can lay eternally with you in my arms
Lets rise from the depths of the ocean
So that we can enjoy the light of day!

Sweet Memories

Sweet, sweet memories
Of a love
That was meant to be
But your heart
You hid from me
Now you got me
Singing this melody
of those
Sweet, sweet memories

Kiss Me

Kiss me, and be mine
Like you kissed me
When you kissed me
For the first time!

Unforgettable

She was a beauty queen
Something beautiful
Than I've ever seen
So unforgettable

Eternity

On the crossroad of heaven and hell
I'll choose you with my dying wish
It takes us centuries to complete a single kiss
Flowers die before we complete a hug
The world will crumble before I tire of this
Our souls will die when we finally reach our bliss!

Is Certain

I love this feeling
The sickness inside
What's most appealing
Is knowing I'll die
Nothing can save me
Nor thee!

That's Life

Life can seem rough
You give it your all
And it's never enough
So on God you call
And He commands you to stand tough!

Love's Quest

What can stop this heart from beating?
What makes it sing?
Flying above
Clouds of pure love
Why does this heart smile everyday?
It will not stray
For its been found
Dug up from the ground
How can I not ask all these questions
Of love's notions
The answer is true
Cause, I love you!

Forever

When does see you later
Becomes good-bye forever?
Separated is the connection
Hearts are breaking
Joy turns to pain
Only memories remain
Tear stained faces
From heart's empty spaces
Letting go is the hardest
Holding on is selfish
Forever becomes a lie
Cause it's time for good-bye!

Fate

Joined in body, mind, and spirit
Equally the kingdoms ours to inherit
Salat is another form of prayer
Universally all who speak They hear
Salvation is offered to those who bear witness to
Allah, Adonai, Jesus, Ra, or whatever inspires you
Nirvana is not only a state of mind
Deafness gives sight to the blind
All beliefs and practices lead to the same path
Long or short anyway you do the math
Love, peace, and unity over greed and hate
Armageddon doesn't have to be our fate
Hurry, and join hearts before it's too late!

Keep Your Head Up

When your heart is heavy
Your shoulder's can't bare anymore
You want to fall on your knee
Inside out you feel sore
Everything around you is a catastrophe
That's when you reach into your core
Scream out like a banshee
Like a strong, courageous lion; roar
Face your problems, never flee
Challenge the bullshit like a matador
Your mind is a master key
Use it to open a desired door
There's absolutely nothing you can't be
Belief in yourself you must restore
Although the future you can't see
Success is never really for sure
Failure isn't a permanent guarantee
You've done well when there's an encore
Until the day your soul is free
Keep your head up, spread your wings and soar
You have to work hard for immortality
If you want your name to live forevermore
Travel bravely through the dark of night
To see and feel the sun's light!

Butterfly

Watch her
As she glides by
An angel's daughter
That beautiful butterfly

Watch her
A flying utopia
A true adventurer
That beautiful mariposa

Watch her
A gentle amazon
Earth's divine prisoner
That beautiful papillon

See her
A rose in the sky
Flutter, flutter, flutter
My beautiful, beautiful butterfly

Our Summer

O'Summer, O'Summer
Where have you gone?
Days like nights of winter
Though the sun shines on
O'My Lord, O'My Lord
Why did you take our Summer?
Summer is now your reward
We're left with "why?" to ponder
No more of Summer's rays
We'll never again see Summer's smile
The end of Summer's days
Good-bye Summer, our chile
Blessed be our Summer, blessed be
Be free O'Summer, be free.

(Elegy to Summer Thompson <10/22/2009>)

Steel My Heart

I walk around
My head down
With nowhere to go

In my town
I'm just a clown
No one says hello

I try to stall
The tears that fall
Running down my face

No one at all
Hears my call
Cause their in outer space

When will it heal
The pain I feel
That's breaking my heart

With the Devil I'll deal
For a heart of steel
That will never fall apart!

Do You Believe

Do you believe in magick?
The Goddess?
Were-rabbits?
The living forest?
Gnomes?
Faeries?
Mystical tomes?
Floating berries?
Dragon tales?
Pixie dust?
Elf delivered mail?
Pegasus?
The spirits of the east?
Cinderella's dress
Beauty and the Beast?
The spirits of the west?
Astaroth?
The spirits of the south?
The spirits of the north?
Speaking without the mouth?
Flying carpets?
Genies?
Talking poppets?
Harpies?
All you can imagine?
Do you believe that it's all happening?

Love Song

Sing to me
Of simpler things
Set me free
With a ring
Light my candle
With internal fires
Grip my handles
digging deep for desires
Kiss the hearts
Inside our soul
Once it starts
We lose control
Love won't stop
Now from the top
Sing to me
And set me free!

Reminiscing

"Let me perm your hair,
It will make your waves better!"
Why did I let that nonsense in my ear
You had me looking like a white surfer
But I've given you your share
Telling the whole Price Chopper you're on crack
I wonder what they thought when we left there
Probably that I took you outside for more slaps
Or how I used to let the oldies blare
I never knew that used to get you pissed
When I fell down the stairs you didn't care
So fuck you too, you fat slutty bitch
When I needed love you were always here
I love you and my kids with eternal bliss
I know me not being there isn't fair
All you got to do is just reminisce!

I Got Nothing But Love

I've no diamonds
No pearls
I've not the riches
Of the worlds
What I've got
Is proven and true
I've nothing
But love for you

I've no castle
No throne
I've not a bed
To lay in a home
I've only this heart
You have the key to
I've nothing
But eternal love for you

I've no gifts
No curse
I've not the sun
Moon, stars, nor universe
What I've got isn't fake
It's real and natural
I've nothing
But undying love for you!

Let Me Count The Ways

How many times I've told you to believe
I told you before I would never leave
How many times I've told you we're true love
I told you before the rest we're above
How many times I told you I'm all yours
I told you before I'd give you the shores
How many times I've told you stop trying
I told you before your satisfying
How many times I've told you you're all mines
I told you before you're why my sun shines
How many times I've told you don't ask why
I told you before cause you're my night sky
How many times I've told you to trust me
I told you before love is loyalty
How many times I've told you to just smile
I told you before we'll walk down that aisle
How many times I've told you you're special
I told you before always I'll love you!

That's Love

Cold hearted love
Riding on a wingless dove
Wet tears fall like dried blood
But that's love, that's love

Brighter than a dark moon
Shinier than a rusted spoon
More secured than a opened cocoon
But that's love, that's love!

What You Know?

I can tell you a million ways
How good a woman's love feels
But you won't know until that day
When you know it to be real
Do you know my feelings better than me?
After my life fell from the shelf
Do you have special powers of empathy?
You don't need to feel it for yourself
You know what's it like to be poor?
Or what's it like to be rich?
Doesn't matter if you're either or
Don't answer unless you've been through it
Everybody lives to die
That's just the way it goes
Don't knock what you haven't given a try
We can only speak on what we know!

More Than Words

Sincere words are spoken
Still it doesn't seem real
Hearts aren't capable of verbal expression
So how do I say what I feel?
Feelings expressed with precision
I try, but come up with nil
My words are but an adumbration
Unable to imitate my heart's trill
Your beauty deserves perfect adulation
Worshipped with unyielding zeal
You are God's heavenly creation
How do I let you know my will?
Beyond words, but through actions
With more than words I shall reveal?

Immortal

Watch the young get old
Embrace a dying rose a million days
Story of your life never told
Even if written a trillion ways
Do you want to live forever
Forever and ever?

Know all there is to know
Worshipped as being divine
Seen all this world has to show
Nights where stars no longer shine
Do you want to live forever
Forever and ever?

Questioning if the universe feels pain
Witnessing enough blood to fill the oceans
On Earth as it begins to wane
Eventually completely stopping it's motions
Do you really want to live forever
Forever and ever and ever?!

A 9-Ton Diamond

Never hate
Never be a snake
Never ever rat
Guess I don't have to tell you that
Never follow another's lead
Unless they have a jewel you need
Never try, just do it
Whatever you dream, pursue it
Never be a quitter
Life isn't all sweet, it's also bitter
Never give someone your word
Then treat it less than a gram of turd
Never fear Cupid's arrow
Take risks, that's how you grow
Never be content with being a mortal
The whole world should be at your funeral
Always be real in everything you do
Never change, stay true to you!

Onederful

In life
Sometimes two
Becomes one
And that one
Becomes something
Awesome
Looking at you two
I see
One beautiful heart
I see
One amazing life
Always ready to start
I see
What may in the world
Will never have the pleasure
Of seeing
I see
One true love
Shared between
A onederful being

Sold Soul

You sold your soul
For nothing in return
Giving up full control
Refusing to remain taciturn
Looking at your reflection
Do you see a man?
After a thousand resurrections?
Or another member of the Klan
The enemy is not your friend
They want your inside help
Until you meet your end
No one will hear your yelp
Your heart is filled with hate
A torturous death is your fate!

Just My Imagination

Remembering the time
When I believed you were mine
All mines
Happiness so sweet
It made me laugh in my sleep
Know what it's like to laugh in your sleep?
Minutes turned to eternity
Looking at love between we
I mean, love between you, and me
Taking it further
Introducing our sons and daughter
Your sons and daughter

Lights! Camera! Action! Cut!

Unconditional trust
Making plans for only us
All of us
A cruel deception
Thinking true love was your intention
But L.O.V.E. was always your intention
True heartache
For the first time ever I felt my heart break
Have you ever felt your heart truly break?
Lifted veil from blind eyes
Seeing everything you said was lies
Lies on top of lies on top of lies
Love's school
I'll never pass, cause I'm a fool
I'll always be love's fool
The curtain's contraction
After watching the beautiful actress in action

Lights! Camera! Action! Cut!

I Love You

I love your smile
I love the way you kiss
I love your style
I love how you do that and this
I love your ebony eyes
I love your hairs and mole
I love your chocolate thighs
I love your lips and nose
I love your sense of silly
I love the way you talk
I love your (ahem) lily
I love the way you walk
I love your everything
This is only a few
I truly love you
For you!

No Longer

No longer lonely
No longer poor
The heart is no longer stony
Locks are no longer on the door

The sky is no longer gray
Nights no longer cold
Lips no longer have to pray
Lost no longer is the soul

No longer is love without a home
No longer is this day mines
This road of life I no longer travel alone
For we are one in mind, heart, body, soul, love, life at all times!

Don't They Know It's The End

Why does the sun go on shining
Why does the sea still rushes to the shore
Don't they know it's the end of the world?
Cause you don't love me anymore

Why does the birds keep singing
Why does the stars radiate from above
Don't they know it's the end of the world?
Since I lost your love

Why does my heart keep on beating
Why does these tears fall from my eyes
Don't they know it's the end of the world?
Since you said good-bye!

Nobody Cares

Cry if you will
Nobody will hear you
Scream and shout
The world is not paying attention
Your alone in this world
Nobody cares about you
You got unnoticed everywhere
When will it stop
When will they realize
We can't survive without eachother!

End Of Days

We behave like savages
The children of Gods
Disrespecting our Mother
Who bears us on her back
Running killing eachother
No peace, no love, no equality
Our days are coming to an end
When it's over don't you dare ask why
Don't you dare!

Elixir

Bathe in the life of the unclean
Senses become keen
Drip after drip
Life on my lips
Immortality it gives us
So we drink with lust
Ahhh it's so sweet
Honey can't compete
If these wells were ever to dry
Surly I'd cry
Red eyes tears
Of blood filled years!

High On Love

Who needs words
Or herbs
When you heart is singing high

Forget the birds
And the burbs
Our loving is living fly

Pull us apart, never
From a sweet kiss
Like this
That will last forever!

The End

The end is drawing near
Deep in my soul I can feel it
Every memory I'll hold dear
With eyes like a leaky faucet
Ages since I've seen the beauty of your ebony face
Thirty nine beautiful moons
Shined like your smile for my heart to trace
But the end is drawing near soon
Soon my love, soon

The end draws near
I can feel it in my soul
Yet still I shed a lonely tear
For without you I'm not whole
Thirty seven beautiful moons shined
Since I've heard the melody of your voice
Sixty five moons ago our love was combined
But the end draws near without a choice
Without a choice, without a choice

The end is near
And your still on my mind
Tell me, truth or dare?
Truth, your love was and is divine
Sixty six beautiful shining moons ago
I loved you without knowing why
Now it's a hundred and forty three moons later, and I know
But the end is here, so this is good-bye
Good-bye my love, good-bye!

Honesty

I applaud you
For choosing not to deceive
You said your words were true
Now this I wholly believe
Cause lets be honest
Where do lies get us
It's better to confess
If you want someone's trust
Now honestly speaking
I understand the situation
Makes no sense sneaking
And having to use manipulation
I take my hat off to your honesty
Cause you really didn't have to share
But I'm glad you told me
Now I know we're here
To be honest
Your honesty
Honestly
Makes you a good friend
Nothing more honest
Than our honesty
And honestly
I believe we'll last til the end!

My Sweet Granny

How much do I love thee
Let me start counting to infinity
You I place before me
Your unconditional love is no privy
A smile that shines radiantly
Black woman of antiquity
When I did wrong you beat my booty
And that put an end to my foolery
You taught me to be strong mentally
May this ode reach you spiritually
Words can't ever express my love completely
Know that I love you dearly
No one can ever take your place, honestly
Cause you'll always be my dear sweet Granny!

Smile For Me

Ashes to ashes, dust to dust
For now I enter the darkness
Don't cry cause death is a must
Instead let your heart be filled with gladness

My home awaits me with open arms
I shall not look back at my past
It's there for you to remember my charms
Smile for me for I'm free at last

From the dark womb of my mother I came
To the dark womb of Mother Earth I shall return
I'll always be with you just speak my name
In your darkest hour I'm the light that burns

Through your tears I will not manifest
My physical is gone, but I'm here in spirit
Remember the times we had from worse to best
Listen for my voice and you shall hear it

Live your life with your head up high
Fear no path for with you I'll always be
Darkness took me, don't ask why
Just share our memories and just smile for me!

Thank You

You had endured
Nine months of discomfort
My life you insured
With love and support
If I never said it before
Know now it's true
I'll say it a million times more
Mommy, thank you!

You taught me to survive
Out there in the wilderness
Stay strong in my faith as I strive
And our Lord will take care of the rest
If I never told you before
Know now it's true
I'll say it a billion times more
Mommy, thank you!

You define to me what a woman
Is truly suppose to be
God fearing, strong, resilient, loving, unbeaten
And radiating with inner and outer beauty
If I never expressed it before
Know now it's true
I'll say it a trillion times more
Mommy, thank you!

You are my best friend
No thing or body comes between us
Right or wrong I know you'll love me til the end
For our spirits are bonded by perfect love and trust
If I never said it before
Know now it's true
I'll say it my throat gets sore
Mommy, thank you!

Genocide

I'm a poison to my own body
Smoking gun committing suicide
Killing every part of myself slowly
Whites are not it, I am genocide

I rob myself of the little I possess
Flooding my system with drugs, morals aside
Causing myself death I'll never confess
Don't you know, I am genocide

Why do I destroy my own blackness?
Why don't I love what's inside?
Why do I treat myself so heartless?
I guess cause, I am genocide

I put a bullet in my head, and killed my sister
I slit my wrist, and my brother died
I stabbed my heart, and disgraced my ancestors
I don't want to be, but I am genocide!

Tattle Teller

What you thought
That you could stop my flow
Praying I'd get caught
Ha-ha-ha, no, no, no
You work in the dark
Plotting to stop my shine
But I walk away without a mark
Stop hating on mine
Your always informing the devil
Watching and listening to others
Their down fall you revel
You'll never be my brother
Families you destroy
With the point of a finger
Nothing but a good ol' boy
With the pigs you linger
How long will you hide
In that little dark hole
Surely you have no pride
After you sold your soul
You live on your knees
So you'll die on your head
Your master won't hear your pleas
When your blood is shed
Cowards die a million deaths
How many lives do you have left?!

Mother (Home)

Through your existence
I came into existence
Through your love
I was born

For without you
There would be no me
For without you
My soul would've never been set free

How can I thank you?
For there's not enough words
So how can I thank you?
When there's not enough time

Your beauty none could match
Only one you, never a batch
Your style and grace is truly supreme
I'm a Prince for you're a Queen

I was robbed of life
When your's was taken
Stabbed in my heart with the bluntest knife
That was the feeling of my heart breaking

Although I know your always here with me
Watching and protecting me from your throne
My mind and heart is where you'll forever be
For in your loving arms is truly my home!

Not Yet

Thinking of the times
Wondering where they've gone
Convicted of uncommitted crimes
My freedom fights to be born
Assassination attempts on what's mines
Fighting darkness until dawn
Higher my iron will climbs
Unwary, unbeatable, fearless, strong
Unconquerable is my mind
Breakable are my bones
Unceasingly swimming through slime
Until I reach my home
They say give up the fight
For you'll never escape the net
I'll carry on with all my might
The grave I'm destined to go
But not yet, not yet!

Family

From mother and father
Came brother and sister
To me family matters
There's no love that's greater

Families always have ups
Families always have downs
Our blood is from the same cup
Heirs from the same crown

From holidays to birthdays
From best days to worse days
We're family everyday
Though we're different in our own ways

Family, what does it mean to you?
Family means everything to me
One fact remains true
No matter what we'll always be family!

What's Love

When you'd do anything for someone
Even endure the worst kind of pain
When you just know they're the one
You feel them in your soul, heart, and brain

When it's impossible to walk away
Even when they've broken your heart
When your given strength to stay
Forgive and move on to a new start

When you feel you've been betrayed
Yet they still have your trust
When you feel like your heart been slayed
Still standing even though you've been crushed

When somehow they've been unfaithful
You refuse to play the payback game
When after they say I love you
You believe, cause you still feel the same

When your strong enough to realize
Not even true love is perfect
When you can wipe the pain from ya'll lives
Cause you know they're truly worth it!

Pocket Full Of Promises

How much is a promise worth?
Is it more than life at birth?
How much does a promise cost?
Can you buy it with a treasure long lost?

What is the worth of a broken promise?
Is it less than a child's passing wish?
What is the cost of a promise broken?
Can you buy it with a wooden token?

What is the worth of a lie everyone believes is true?
How much would it cost me too tell one to you?

Inseperable

Inseperable
Like colorful leaves
And the fall
Like cement
And a wall
Like beautiful flowers
And the spring
We're inseparable
Like ...
Well everything!

Forgiveness

I gave you all my love
And you just took advantage
Had me in a rocket high above
Only so you could do the most damage

How could I ever forgive you
Just why should I?
You promised to be 110% faithful
And that was just a lie

Never did I imagine
You would break my heart
With my heart and soul I was all in
But it seems you were playing the part

Just why should I forgive?
Cause deep down I know you truly love me
Without you I could never live
Now our love will be all it can be

For this pain I know you apologize
Now let us grow to our very best
So wipe these tears from our eyes
Love, you have my true forgiveness!

Love Conquers All

Hearts may break
But just don't shatter
It's how strong is the glue and tape
In the end that matters

Will it ever heal
Will the pain ever stop
Will it ever feel
Will this baggage I'll ever drop

I can't let go
I don't ever want to lose you
Though I'm feeling low
I know this love is true

Love conquers all
Even the pain of betrayal
Love will stand tall
When all else fails!

Give Me Foreva

Why when your given something good
The Gods want to take it away
Wouldn't understand it if I could
Why bother getting on our knees and pray
Give me back my end
Give me back my start
Give me back my friend
Give me back my heart

All the smiles, laughter and good times
Aren't the best things in life free?
Then taken away as punishment for crimes
Tears and broken hearts pay the hidden fee
Give me back my sunset
Give me back my moonshine
Give me back my Romeo and Juliet
Give me back my forevermore mine

Love can't leave us now
The best part has yet to come
Can't just send us crashing down
We've only just begun
So give me back my sky above
Give me back my nirvana
Give me back my true love
Please, just give me back my foreva!

Please

Please love don't go
Please don't walk away
Please give us a chance to grow
Please I'm begging you to stay

Please don't turn your back on us
Please don't let our love down
Please don't take away your trust
Please love not now

Please don't cause us pain
Please don't sever our heart and soul
Please we have so much to gain
Please just let love take control

Please love don't you love me
Please love you know our love is true
Please love don't take away our eternity
Please love please I'm begging you

Please don't make our soul's cry
Please love don't let love die!

Amaze Me

I'm down on my knees
Send your smile to lift me high
Amaze me

The pain has my eyes watery
Show me that star in your eye
Amaze me

My heart's bleeding hear its plea
Give it wings and make it fly
Amaze me

My soul is lost somewhere dark and lonely
Come bring it the light that is you and I
Amaze me

Please amaze me baby
Like you've done countless times before
I need you to amaze me
Please, just once more!

Can I Show You

Can I show you how beautiful you are
How your amazing smile defines true beauty
How your eyes possess the brightest star
Can I show you what I see?

Can I show you how you make flowers grow
How you give birds their melody
How you rain summer when there's snow
Can I show you what I see?

Can I show you how your so strong
How you single handedly hold together a family
How you miraculously right every wrong
Can I show you what I see?

Can I show you how you own my heart and soul
How you make loving you so easy
How you complete me and make me whole
Can I show you what you are to me?

Can I give you love that's true
Can I just show you, you?!

My Black Diamond

Flawless
I find no wrong in you
Inside and out your perfectly beautiful

Priceless
Nothing could ever match your worth
You are truly the rarest jewel to exist on Earth

Black
The color of skin, soul, and pride
That Goddess that radiates from inside

Diamond
Your a strong, beautiful black woman
The way you sparkle is absolutely amazing!

Miles Away

I'm whispering in your ear
Your cuddled in my embrace
Though I'm here and not there
It still feels like we're face to face
A gentle caress of the lips
Passion heats up our hearts
I'm enslaved under chains and whips
Same world though our bodies are in different parts
Take my hand and the unseen becomes seen
Close your eyes and just believe
We're together taking in a beautiful scene
With love there's nothing we can't achieve
We're not physically in eachothers presence
But our souls have found their own way
They have their own special resilience
We're one heart, soul and love, even when we're miles away!

My Queen

Can you really be?
A living, breathing fantasy
Before me as a reality
My eyes you must deceive
For you are beyond lovely
A single rose conquering beauty
Your eyes set my soul free
I wonder if I am worthy
Do I deserve to worship thee?
In my life you fit wonderfully
With me no woman will come before ye
To you I pledge my loyalty
My queen longed to receive
King and Queen sharing love's majesty!

The Wait Is Over

How dare I keep her waiting
When it's I she longs to hold
How dare I keep her waiting
When she possesses my soul
How dare I call this living
When my heart has begun to rot
How dare I stay away from her
When she's my all and all
How dare I stay away from her
When I can hear her call
How dare I keep her waiting
When she's the who, what and why I live for
How dare I keep her waiting
I can't and I won't, not a second more!

I Can't Stop Thinking Of You

Through my mind
Your running in and out, out and in
From the start of my day
Til its very end

Your even in my dreams
Taking my hand and leading the way
Showing me things I never dreamed of
As you beg me to stay

Someone is on the radio
Singing a love song
While I'm looking in your eyes
Dancing and singing along

Stuck in a deep trance
Visualizing your laughter and smile
I've been missing all of you
For the longest while

I'll never stop thinking of you
I could write an endless poem
I reluctantly stop here
Lest my thoughts never reach your home!

Still On My Mind

I lost my mind
And you found it
Now you don't want to give it back

Your in it all the time
You have it completely surrounded
Even the tiny little crack

Every single day and night
From moonshine to sunshine
Every-breathe-I-Take

Your in my sight
Isn't mind evasion a crime?
All the while giving me this pleasurable ache!

Damn You (still thinking!)

What took you so long
To come and take me
And steal my mind and heart away
Never knew love could be so strong
Leaving me only one plea
Don't ever leave, in my mind forevermore stay!

Your Day

Today is your day
Only for you the sun shines

Today is your day
For you the stars will align

Today is your day
Only for you the nightingales will sing

Today is your day
For you diamonds will sparkle on a ring

Today is your day
Only for you the sky glows blue

Today is your day
Only for me and world, nothing matters but you!

Adults Only

I watch as the sweat drips off your sexy smooth body
You mean, you want more of these pleasures I'm giving your pussy
Up and down as tour titties bounce with your animal movements
Winding and grinding begging for more of my dick's treatment
Screams of pure pleasure and pain echoes in this room
Ride this delicious dick, like a witch riding a broom
You collapse in orgasm, covering my balls in your pussy's juice
Breathing is uncontrollable and heavy as your tight walls begin to loose
I take control of your body as I roll you under me
You feel my long dick deep in you as I fuck you silly
Sucking on your soft titties with its hard nipples in my mouth
Fuck me, you command as my dick slides out and in, in and out
Switching positions as you poke your beautiful ass in the air
I grab hold of your hips as I fuck you, and then start pulling your hair
You scream out my name, begging for mercy with an erotic moan
Damn this pussy feels good, is what you hear me groan
Harder and faster I massage your pussy as I'm about to cum
You pull away and turn around and suck my dick using your tongue
Damn woman, you swallow every last single drop
Still sucking my dick hungrily, you don't want to stop
Your a nasty girl, you know just how I love it
I slap you on the ass, now go make me some chicken and biscuit
You better make it quick, you little slut
I'm ready to fuck you in that tight ass butt
Your wishes is my command, damn woman you know how to please
As soon as I finished wiping my hands, you are already on your hands
and knees
Woman your my every wish cum true, I'll never kick you to the curb
Now wait your sexy ass there, as I put the sign on the door - Do Not
Disturb!

After Hours

The atmosphere is humid
From the combined heat
Hearts beat rapid
With a jungle beat
Smell of a rose
Fills the air
Exotic scent to the nose
From the middle of nowhere
A peach is offered freely
It's moist sweetness pleases
Tongue licks it savioringly
As it slowly teases
The moon's dew
Quenches the thirst
Closed lids eyes see through
The gift and the curse

Forbidden Dance

Candle light dances
Off entangled bodies
True romance is
Moved with a cloud's ease
Caresses that explore
Moist - dark - sweet - treasures
Tongue opens the door
That's filled with pleasures
Time is suddenly frozen
With waves of bliss
The right moment is chosen
To give the vibrating kiss
Air is charged with passion
As the hunger is fed
Bodies joined in a fashion
That rocks the bed
Fire burning within
Melting a chocolate mix
Hear the incoming explosion
That will transfix
Locked in a trance
From the forbidden dance!

Royal Pleasure

Close the blinds, lock the door
Disconnect the phone
Time to get what you've been longing for
It's just us finally all alone
Lit scented candles add the spice
As the slow jamz fill the room
Grab the whipped cream and bucket of ice
Now prepare to have your passions consumed
I peel the clothes off your skin
Kissing you while in my embrace
Lay you down and put my face within
As I inhale, kiss, taste
Your desire is burning hot
I need to cool it down a bit
Ice on tongue, licking your spot
You cum as I'm savoring your clit!

Howling Love

As the wolf sings to the moon
My heart also sings a tune
Filled with laughter and joy
About love between a girl and a boy
Surely as the sun will rise
I'll sing of the stars in your eyes
Your like a moon in my mind way above
Got me down here howwwwwling for your love!

Love Always

There's so much I want to
Tell you that's on my mind
Give this limited
Amount of time
I'll just tell you the most
Important one of all
I'll always love you
Winter, spring, summer, fall!

Sugar Love

Sweet was the night
I laid eyes on you
Sweet was the sound
one I never knew
Blessed was your touch
Putting fire in my soul
blessed is your love
Bright and whole!

Fallen Star

Falling from a star
Now I'm lost
I don't know where you are
Everyday
I search near and far
Every night
I dream of your heart
Until that time
I'll look for you amongst the stars!

Scent From Heaven

She smelled like a rose
In full bloom
On a cold winter day
Sugar to the nose
In a room
Filled with a summer ray!

Eternal Duet

From day one
That moment when our eyes met
Life was done
And eternity started for this duet!

Now It's Time

Now as I begin
To wash you off my skin
I'm going to peel you away
Cause your not right within

Soulmate

The fire that burns in my soul is strong
It wants you, needs you whether it's right or wrong
I think about you constantly without pause
I think about your smile randomly, just because
Do you feel this way about me?
Do you want, need, dream of us soon to be
I don't know what exactly calls my attention to these feelings
Your words, your charm, your you, it's my heart your stealing
Although I've never layed eyes on your physical beauty
Inside I don't care for that, cause your beautiful on the inside to me
Give us a chance to travel to unseen and unknown worlds together
Give our hearts a chance to become one, and purer than Maat's feather
I can read the dictionary, and won't find a that defines how I feel
Only our souls can give words to our feelings, only they can reveal
I want to spend eternity with us, I never want us to take a break
Call me crazy if you like, but I know without a doubt your my soulmate!

Infatuation

Woman don't you know what you do to me?
I'm your cherry red Porsche only you can drive me crazy lady
You say your not, but I think you are
For what sane woman would have the keys to this car
Don't you know all your words move me beyond reality
It's unreal the way they enslave my mind and heart, verbally
Looking in your eyes takes me to places unseen
The beauty I see I don't even see in my dreams
The very scent of you sends me levitating to the furtherest star
Your always right there no matter where I go or how far
Woman your body taste like the sweetest pleasures reserved for the Gods
After tasting your heavenly delights, to live with you would be really hard
I've been touched by a Goddess, and a Goddess I've touched
My hands will never tire of caressing your body, no such thing as too much
Woman through love, you possess my mind, body, heart and soul
There's not one cell, one atom that your love does not control
You say I'm infatuated, lady with you I'm beyond infatuation
The love that you have, gives my mind, body, heart and soul pure
satisfaction!

Right Now

I've been waiting to be with you for only
The Gods know how long
Traveling from planet to planet, everywhere in this
Universe for my love so strong
Now your in my life once again
Making me smile like a clown
I don't want to wait to hold you
Any longer I want you now
Not now, but right now
Us finding eachother again
Took life times to accomplish
Never will I leave, never will I share my love
I'm actually proud to be selfish
The tears of longing you cry
That come rolling down
Tells me you don't want to wait to feel my touch
You want to feel it now
Not now, but right now
Our days and nights are filled
With constant thoughts of love for eachother
We're missing eachother everyday and every night
Desiring, wanting, needing our lover
We see eachother in our dreams
Hugging and kissing, arms wrapped tightly around
This waiting is killing us slowly
We need to explore our love now
Not now, but right now
As above so below
Our love will forever shine brightly amongst the stars
For I know no love in this universe
Except the God and Goddess, that compares to ours

The day will come
When we'll submerge to the abyss of our love and drown
This love is so strong
You want me, I want you, we want us now
Not now, but right now
Fear is something I never knew
Until I fell in love with you all over again
I can't begin to imagine a day
Without you, my soulmate, my lover, my friend
If death came and claimed you today
Life would have no meaning that is sound
I wouldn't want to wait until tomorrow
To be with you again, but today, this moment, now
Not now, but right now
Right now!

Get To Know You

I'm taking this time to write you this letter
Asking to be a friend who can take your bads and make them better
I want to know what like, dislike and everything in between
What disappoints you, inspires you, whats your nightmares, your dreams
Can we share secrets and promise never to tell another
Know your secrets will be safe with me, for I won't even tell my mother
I want to be the friend you think about when you need to smile
No matter what we go through, good or bad, it will be all worthwhile
Now with all that said and done, know that these words are true
I sincerely just want to get to know you!

If This Be My Last

If this be my last poem
I pray, a young mind it will inspire
If these be my last written words
I pray, they be used to feed a fire

If this be my last stand
I pray, it's to free the mind of slaves
If this be my last fight
I pray, it's the one my Blackness craves

If this be my last prayer
I pray, I'll finally get an answer
If this be my last wish
I pray, it rids the world of it's cancer

If this be my last sunset
I pray, I'll finally get life's meaning
If this be my last night
I pray, these inner voices stop screaming

If this be my last cry
I pray, it'll ease the pain of a nation
If this be my last teardrop
I pray, it'll be enough for libation

If this be my last meal
I pray, it'll end world hunger
If this be my last sip of water
I pray, it'll make the desert weary stronger

If this be my last high
I pray, I see the world from better angles
If this be my last cup of demon piss
I pray, I drink it in the company of angels

If this be my last copulation
I pray, love is left to be born again
If this be my last kiss
I pray, it be given to a true friend

If this be my last journey
I pray, I land in the arms of my Mother
If this be my last step
I pray, someone follows to take one further

If these be my last words
I pray, every last one be declared true
If this be my last breath
I pray, I'm close enough to give it to you

If this simply be my last
I pray, on this world I leave a mark
If this really be my end
I pray, I live on in my nation's heart

Contact Author

I would love to hear from you, please don't hesitate
all of your opinions are welcomed
whether they be good or bad, happy or sad.

Kayson Pearson
#04-A-4176
P.O.Box 1187
Alden, New York 14004-1187

or by email
Kaysonpearson@gmail.com
Facebook: kayson pearson (Love is Life)

Printed in the United States
by Baker & Taylor Publisher Services